W9-BTC-328

ONE FOR ME, ONE FOR YOU

Little Ideas for Caring for Yourself and the World

EVA OLSEN   ILLUSTRATED BY KAT KALINDI

CASTLE POINT BOOKS
NEW YORK

This kindness space belongs to:

_____

_____

CONTENTS

Be kinder to yourself.
And then let your kindness
flood the world.

—PEMA CHÖDRÖN

Welcome to a Kinder World

DO YOU FEEL TORN BETWEEN THINKING ABOUT THE NEEDS OF OTHERS AND FINDING WAYS TO FILL YOUR OWN NEEDS? Thank you, you beautiful human. Compassionate connection may be the key to healing our world and moving forward in hope.

To keep spreading good deeds like apple seeds we must take a few moments to water our own tree, too. We know this, at heart, but being other-oriented can make it hard to imagine where to begin. We may even feel we don't *need* care, but we do. When we practice self-care, we center ourselves, we recharge, and we project a positive energy that's tough to conjure when we're overextended or run-down.

The good news is, you don't need to choose between self-care and caring for the world. *One for Me, One for You* helps you discover the perfect balance. In each spread you'll find some simple activities to do for yourself, followed by complementary ideas for turning them outward. As you find ones that resonate, add them to your routine, so you can keep being the beautiful human you were meant to be.

For Me

YOUR SOUL WON'T HAVE THE SPACE TO BLOOM WHEN IT'S TRAPPED INDOORS ALL DAY. Set an appointment with yourself to breathe in fresh air and savor the wonder of nature—whether that looks like enjoying your morning coffee outdoors while listening to the birds or taking a walk through the park at lunchtime.

For You

THINK OF SOMEONE WHO MAY NOT BE ABLE TO PHYSICALLY EMBRACE THE OUTDOORS TODAY, maybe due to an illness or a crazy work schedule. Bring them a touch of nature through a flower delivery (professionally arranged or backyard-picked), a beautiful outdoor photo emailed or texted, or another way to experience healing from nature.

For Me

BOOKS CAN BE LIFE CHANGING. So why are you putting off picking up that novel with great reviews or the cover that speaks to you? Go for it—today. Purchase the book or borrow it from the library. Then block out some reading time—even for just a few pages—and enjoy the journey into another time, place, or perspective.

For You

GO THROUGH YOUR BOOKSHELVES AND CHOOSE A BOOK TO SHARE with a friend—complete with a note explaining why it made you think of the recipient. Or donate a few titles to your local library. If you're handy and inspired, you might even build a book-sharing box for your neighborhood and populate it with a few of your own books.

For Me

TODAY IS A PERFECT DAY TO OPEN A DOOR TO A NEW OPPORTUNITY. If you have been wanting to sign up for a class or learn a new skill—whether business, barre, improv, or hand lettering—take the first step. Don't label even your craziest goals as silly or unrealistic! Commit to your dreams, double down on you, and see how inspired and refreshed you feel when you start opening those doors.

For You

WHAT DOORS CAN YOU OPEN FOR OTHERS? Consider two people in your life who might benefit from getting to know each other professionally or personally. Introduce them with the hope that their connection might inspire great things on both sides. Can't think of a connection to make? Watch for an opportunity to hold open a door for someone, literally! Kindness can be that simple.

(13)

For Me

WHEN WAS THE LAST TIME YOU TREATED YOURSELF TO SOME PRAISE? Write a letter for your eyes only detailing something you really like about yourself! This is a great way to bolster your self-esteem today, and re-reading it can be a saving grace on days when you're feeling low. Keep it in a secret (but accessible) place.

For You

SEIZE THE OPPORTUNITY TO SHARE AN OUT-OF-THE-BLUE COMPLIMENT with a loved one, coworker, neighbor, or service worker you encounter in your day. Bolstering words don't need an occasion. Instead, consider your appreciation a way to bring joy and energy that may fuel another person through their day—and fill their tank before it even becomes empty.

For Me

IF YOU'VE BEEN SAVING YOUR PENNIES FOR A RAINY DAY, now is a great time to roll them up. Counting coins can be a soothing and legitimately rewarding task. Look under car seats, in pockets, and in junk drawers. Think of it as a modern-day treasure hunt! Tally up the coins, then treat yourself to a small pick-me-up—it can be anything from a facial mask or candle to a lottery ticket or pack of crayons.

For You

SPARK POSITIVE CHANGE, A LITTLE AT A TIME: Pay for the coffee of the person behind you, pop a few quarters into someone's parking meter, or leave some coin rolls at a laundromat. Another option: wait till you get a tidy sum (like $20) and use it to support a child's school or charity fundraiser.

For Me

"LIKE" IT OR NOT, SOCIAL MEDIA IS A BIG PART OF OUR LIVES. To make sure your accounts reflect who you are, do a social media cleanup. First, think of five words that describe you and your values, then use them as guides to decide if your posts, likes, follows, and friends are in sync. Also, feel free to take a break from social media entirely now and then—no explanations needed.

For You

THINK ABOUT THE ARTISTS, ADVOCATES, NONPROFITS, AND COMPANIES THAT MAKE YOUR HEART SOAR. Start to follow their accounts more closely, and reshare their best work. That's good for them and the friends on your list. Want to be more of a motivator? Pick an area of interest or expertise and start actively seeking and posting pics, quotes, and links.

REPAIR

For Me

LIFE IS FULL OF LITTLE TO-DOS AND TACKLING JUST ONE CAN BE FREEING. Sew on a button, tighten a loose drawer handle, wipe the tops of the ceiling fan blades, or replace a lightbulb. Many such household tasks can be tackled in minutes, leaving you with a sense of satisfaction that lasts all day (or longer).

For You

REPAIRING SMALL RIFTS IN RELATIONSHIPS CAN BE REWARDING, TOO. If an "I'm sorry" is in order, say it—the sooner, the better. No strife in your life right now? Good for you! Think of someone who could use an extra pair of helping hands around the house and tackle their mending pile or minor repairs.

For Me

WATCHING BABIES OR PETS SLEEP CAN BRING PEACE. Getting your own night of peaceful sleep is even better. If your before-bed routine focuses solely on your toothbrush and smartphone, add some soothing steps. Shut off all screens and dim the lights. Then dab on lavender lotion or take a warm bath. Promise yourself to replace past-their-prime pillows, sheets, and PJs with soft, beautiful fabrics that whisper "rest."

For You

PARENTS ARE SOME OF THE MOST SLEEP-DEPRIVED PEOPLE ON THE PLANET. If you have an empty nest or older kids, choose a lucky young family and offer to put the kids to bed while the grown-ups enjoy alone time. Have young kids of your own? Host a sleepover at your place. The favor is likely to be repaid. As for your old sheets and blankets, take them to an animal shelter, where pets can curl up on them for a nice nap.

Z
Z
Z

STAND

For Me

OUR BODIES WEREN'T MADE TO SIT AROUND ALL DAY, so set a reminder to stand up every hour. Use that time to sip some water, make a phone call, delete junk email, gaze out the window, or tidy your desk. To *really* get the blood flowing, take a walk down the hall or step outside, go up and down stairs, or stretch out your tension.

For You

LEARN HOW TO STAND UP FOR MARGINALIZED GROUPS. Don't place the burden of teaching on already overwhelmed or hurting people. Do your own reading or join a change-focused group or committee. Amplify voices on social media by sharing their memes, messages, photos, and professional work. And if anyone says something inappropriate, let them know you won't stand for it.

For Me

REFRAMING OLD ART AND PHOTOS CAN ENLIVEN YOUR SPACE, while retaining the works you love. Even easier, switch them around to different hooks. Reframing opportunities come with emotions, too. Try reframing nervousness by labeling it as excitement. Your body's response to both emotions is the same (your heart and brain are gearing up for action), but a positive label may help change your outlook.

For You

WE OFTEN COME ACROSS UNWANTED ITEMS AS WE REDECORATE (OR DUST). Keep a donation box in a closet to add to along the way. Offer unwanted heirlooms to your family. Save valuables for charity auctions. Donate the rest to a thrift store with a mission you support. Want to preserve the memory of certain pieces? Take a photo—it lasts forever.

LOVE

Reframe

For Me

EVERYONE IS A GUEST ON EARTH. That's why every face-to-face visit is something to be cherished. One way to celebrate each in-person connection: start a guest book. Pick a pretty journal or notebook and set it out at every get-together—no matter how casual. Choose a visitor to be the day's scribe, and ask them to add a statement, food review, silly sketch, or whatever they like.

For You

THANK MOTHER EARTH FOR HER HOSPITALITY by adding to your sustainability practices. That may mean saying no to plastic straws, placing reusable shopping bags in your car, and buying more organics. If you enjoy being outdoors, you might help clean up a local waterway, park, or highway. That's also a good way to meet like-minded friends.

For Me

WATER CAN BE SUCH A SIMPLE BUT REFRESHING GIFT TO YOURSELF. Enroll in an aquacise or stand-up paddleboarding class. Soak in a hot tub. Dance in the rain. Or simply fill a bowl with warm suds, soak your hands in it, and *relax*. Also, don't forget to refill your water bottle often. Hydration is vital for keeping your physical and mental energy flowing.

For You

ALTHOUGH YOU MAY WANT TO LIMIT PLASTICS, IT CAN BE AN ACT OF KINDNESS to stock a few bottles of water in the fridge for landscapers or repair people. Local schools also may benefit from a donated case of water or two for their band, theater, or sports teams. You can offer to collect the "empties" to make sure they get recycled.

CREATE

Crayon

Crayon

For Me

COLORING IS NO LONGER A KIDS-ONLY ACTIVITY. If you vividly remember the joy (and scent) of a new box of crayons, you're the target market for adult coloring books. Filling empty spaces with rich hues creates a state called *flow*, where time and stress melt away. So, treat yourself to a fresh book and the coloring tools of your choice—and don't worry about staying within the lines.

For You

HAVE A COLLECTION OF ODDS AND ENDS FROM BYGONE CRAFT PROJECTS? Choose a kids' club, day center for seniors, or grade-school teacher to bless with your extras. Gifted at art? Offer lessons in your favorite medium—whether officially or just for friends. Or reflect on the artisans who first taught *you*, then send them an out-of-the-blue "thank-you."

For Me

LIFE CAN BE A REAL PRESSURE COOKER. This week, sit down to a meal and truly savor every bite. Use *all* of your senses, not just taste. Or if you're seeking a bigger step into enjoying the world of food, enroll in a cooking class. Immerse yourself in the experience, and try to enjoy the mistakes as much as the successes.

For You

THERE IS SOMETHING BEAUTIFUL ABOUT FEEDING ANOTHER HUMAN BEING. Babies and adults with physical challenges may need help guiding their utensil to their mouth. A far-flung friend may enjoy a care package of local goodies. Food banks, soup kitchens, and meal-delivery programs may need cooks and servers. These activities are food for the soul, too.

LISTEN

For Me

WHEN YOU'RE A GIVING PERSON, IT'S NATURAL TO WANT TO OFFER WORDS OF COMFORT TO OTHERS. But make sure you seek the comfort you need as well. Write yourself a letter of forgiveness and acceptance for whatever is bringing you down in any way right now. Listen to the words as if a friend were speaking them to you. Or ask a trusted loved one to lend you their ear and words of comfort.

For You

WHEN SOMEONE IN YOUR CIRCLE IS UNUSUALLY QUIET, ASK IF THEY NEED A GOOD LISTENER. Try this: paraphrase what they just said but put it in your own words. This allows the speaker to know you're truly listening—and it often helps them better connect with their own situation and emotions. What if you're dying to offer advice? Ask if they want your two cents before chiming in.

For Me

"NO" IS SUCH A TINY WORD, BUT IT'S SO HARD FOR SOME OF US TO SAY! If that sounds like you, try this: Answer all requests with "Let me get back to you." Then check your calendar and gauge your gut reaction before you answer. If you do say yes, you want to make sure you can follow through and feel good about it.

For You

PEOPLE'S CIRCUMSTANCES CHANGE OVER TIME, so let them know you *will* take no for an answer, even if they previously said yes. Are you one of those people who never ask for help? Try to reach out more. Humans are wired to take pleasure in helping one another. Don't deprive your friends of that endorphin rush!

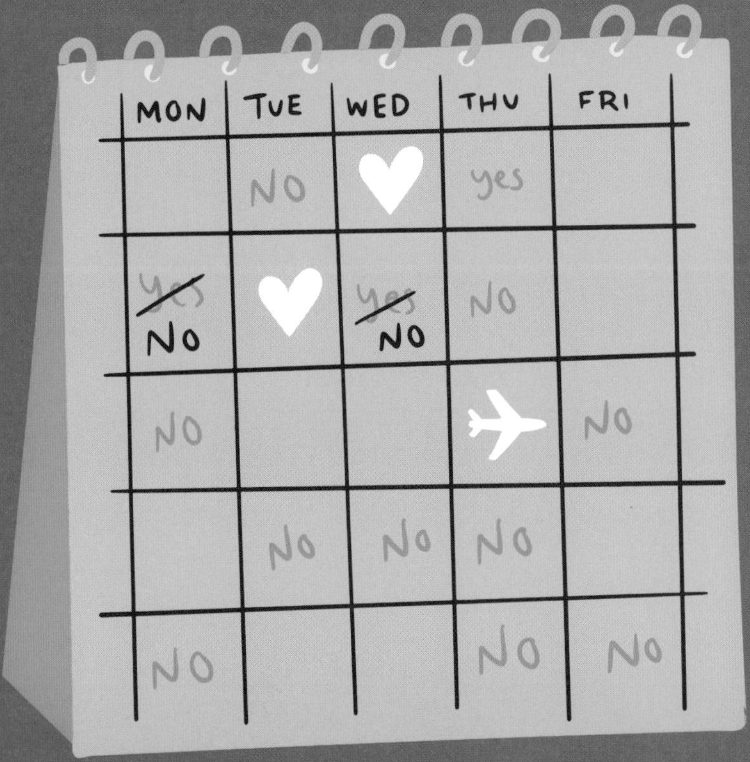
MON
TUE
WED
THU
FRI
NO
yes
~~yes~~ NO
~~yes~~ NO
NO
NO
NO
No
No
No
NO
NO
No

hero

For Me

STRIKING A SUPERHERO POSE CAN MAKE YOU FEEL MORE CONFIDENT IN THE MOMENT. So why not make good posture a habit? Some tricks to reset your body: Roll your shoulders back, and tuck your tummy in. Also pretend you just smelled something stinky. This last move counters *tech neck*, which comes from hunching over a screen all day.

For You

GIVE REAL-WORLD HEROES KUDOS. Hang a "thank-you" sign on your door for delivery people. Double the tip the next time you dine out. Take a hot meal to your local firehouse or ambulance corps—or support their next fundraiser. Bring flowers to a nurses' station. Write an online review for a local service business. Or join Operation Shoebox to donate to the troops.

For Me

IT'S AMAZING HOW JUST A FEW MINUTES OF TAKING IN A TWINKLING SKY can bring awakening and perspective. If you can't catch a clear view of the night sky from your home, drive to the countryside some evening—maybe when there's a meteor shower due. Or plan your next trip in a "dark sky" location. (For ideas, search "astrotourism.")

For You

GIVE THE GIFT OF STARGAZING TO SOMEONE ELSE. Invite a special person in your life to visit a planetarium with you. Send star-show tickets to a child and parent who could use more wonder in their lives. Or make a donation to the astronomy department of a local university.

For Me

BEING GENEROUS WITH AUTHENTIC SMILES CAN IMPROVE YOUR RELATIONSHIPS, your outlook, and maybe even your performance at work. If something is holding you back from grinning big, it's time to address it. To put your best smile forward, baby your teeth with a new toothbrush and regular checkups. Need a few things straightened out? Talk with a cosmetic dentist about options.

For You

SMILES ARE CONTAGIOUS: EVERY TIME YOU SHARE ONE, YOU CAN BRIGHTEN SOMEONE'S DAY. Shine them on strangers and friends alike. And go big or go home! No close-lipped, half-hearted attempts allowed. That way, even if your smile's hidden behind a scarf, people will see your eyes squinch with happiness and kindness.

For Me

IT CAN BE UNCOMFORTABLE ACCEPTING COMPLIMENTS, but it's important to learn to accept them—for your sake and the giver's. Nice shirt! *Thank you!* What a beautiful singing voice! *Thank you!* Great job on that report. *Thank you!* Keep track of these kind words in a journal (in pen or online) and revisit them when you're feeling meh.

For You

GIVING GOOD COMPLIMENTS IS AN ART. To make them meaningful, identify something *specific* you liked and explain *why* you liked it. For example, instead of saying "That dip was *amazing*," you might say, "That dip was so light and creamy. I love how you always introduce me to new dishes! Would you be willing to share your recipe?"

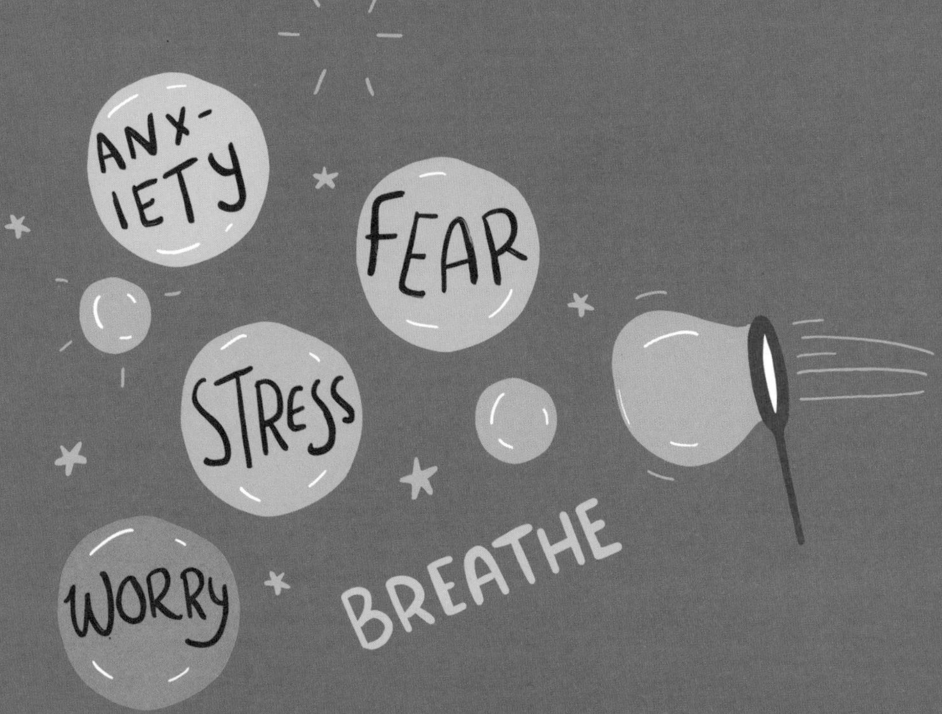
ANX-
IETY
FEAR
STRESS
WORRY
BREATHE

For Me

WHEN YOUR STRESS IS ABOUT TO BUBBLE OVER, TRY THIS: Inhale slowly through your nose for four seconds, hold for two seconds, then exhale through pursed lips for four seconds, as if you were blowing bubbles. Wait two seconds, then repeat. As you do this exercise, imagine you're blowing *real* bubbles, which are carrying your stress far away.

For You

LOOK FOR MINIATURE BOTTLES OF BUBBLES, like those offered as wedding favors, and take a bottle with you wherever you go. Stuck in traffic? Blow bubbles out the window. Need to amuse some bored kiddos? You've got this. Attending a housewarming party? Take them to that, too. Instant mood lightener.

For Me

BONDING WITH FAMILY MEMBERS CAN BE AS EASY AS PIE—or as easy as asking about their famous apple pie. Make a list of questions to ask family members, and record their answers—on video or audio, if they'll allow it. Start a record of newer family traditions, too. One day your sister-in-law's Thanksgiving-night turkey soup will be as legendary as it is delicious.

For You

SHARE WHAT YOU LEARN WITH OTHER FAMILY MEMBERS. You might create your own "family history" book, using scans of old photos, recipes, and articles you've unearthed. Set out a copy at your next family reunion, so everyone can enjoy paging through. Or just email recordings and digital images to interested parties.

FORWARD

For Me

PUT YOUR BEST FOOT FORWARD EVERY DAY! Check the soles of your walking or running shoes. If the tread is worn away in spots, take the shoes to a running store and have a professional measure you for a new pair. They'll assess what amount of cushioning, stability, and other features are best for you. Also, treat yourself to some socks designed to keep feet dry.

For You

WALKING FOR A CAUSE IS A GREAT WAY TO USE THOSE NEW SHOES. There are even virtual 5Ks these days! Instead of throwing out old kicks, give them to a sneaker-recycling program, a charity that refurbishes sneakers, or a shoe store that offers rewards points for donations. (First, tie the pair together so they don't get separated.)

For Me

ENJOYING LOCALLY GROWN FOODS NOT ONLY FEELS *RIGHT*, it can also be better for your body. These fresher foods usually have fewer preservatives and more nutrients. Enjoy them at a farm-to-table restaurant or pick up fresh essentials at the farmer's market. Want to learn more? Plan a "hay-cation" and stay a few days at a working farm.

For You

IF YOUR FRESH FOOD STOCK IS OVERFLOWING, YOU CAN SHARE it with the rest of your community. When you support local farmers, purchase extras to donate to a mission or food bank. Ask if you can donate your time to help harvest or distribute to those in need. Or plant vegetables and herbs in a home or community garden, then share the fruits of your own labor.

HARVEST

For Me

IS THERE SOMETHING—BIG OR LITTLE—THAT'S WEIGHING YOU DOWN? A closure ritual may help. Find a stone, imagine filling it with your troubles, then chuck it into a lake. Or write it all on paper and toss it in a fire, watching it turn to beautiful colors . . . and then to ash. Now you're free to enjoy today and the new beginning that it offers!

For You

WHEN OTHERS ARE HURTING, DON'T TAKE IT PERSONALLY IF THEY DON'T TURN TO YOU. Some people need to talk, while others turtle up. Some seek solace in their faith or a support group. Ask what you can do to help, then respect their wishes. If you see them getting stuck, help them find a mental health professional so they can heal.

For Me

FOR A CHANGE OF PERSPECTIVE, TAKE YOURSELF TO NEW HEIGHTS! Visit the observation deck of a skyscraper, move your desk to a second-floor room, or ride a roller coaster. Hate heights? Do the opposite! Visit a crystal cave or try scuba diving (or snorkeling). For a happy medium, just lie down and watch the clouds roll by.

For You

KNOW SOMEONE WHO'S STUCK IN A RUT? Take them for a Sunday drive or visit a friend in another city. Introduce them to a book or movie they would never choose or play songs from a new music genre. If they nix these ideas, let them pick one. Maybe they'd like your help to rearrange or repaint a room in their home. Any way to liven things up!

SPA-AHH

For Me

MASSAGE BUFFS SAY THIS TREATMENT PUTS THE "AH" IN "SPA." If you're not touchy-feely, there are plenty of other ways to relax. Consider a pedicure or facial, or just get your hair done. (Scalp massages are ah-mazing.) No time? Try a DIY foot massage. Place a tennis ball under your arch and roll it around on the floor. So good!

For You

SOME SPAS HAVE TAKEN THE "GUILTY" OUT OF "GUILTY PLEASURE" by offering packages that allow visitors to donate a portion of the fee to a charity. If your favorite one does not, you could suggest it. Sometimes we can help others just by sparking an idea. Or grow out your hair and donate the locks. This takes some time, but not much effort!

For Me

WHEN'S THE LAST TIME A PROFESSIONAL PHOTOGRAPHER TOOK YOUR PICTURE? Chances are, your social media picture is that old, too! Treat yourself to a session or hire a photography student to do the honors. Update your profile, then download some photo-editing apps and play. You can add bunny ears—or erase laugh lines!

For You

TREAT SOMEONE SPECIAL IN YOUR LIFE TO A PHOTO SESSION. You can hire a pro or try DIY to mark a milestone in their life—whether earning a degree, starting a new job, moving into a first house, or having a baby. Or invite them to squeeze into a photo booth or selfie to celebrate some fun and your relationship. They'll enjoy the time spent together as much as the keepsake results!

*Smile

For Me

IT'S WHAT'S UNDERNEATH THAT COUNTS. That's true of clothing, too. Replacing worn-out undies can make you feel like a million bucks. This time, get *fitted* for a bra instead of buying off the rack, and try something new. Get rid of the stretched-out stuff. You deserve better!

For You

MANY PROGRAMS DONATE UNDIES AND SOCKS TO PEOPLE IN NEED, so when you buy for you, it helps others, too. Want to make a difference locally? Donate diapers or feminine hygiene supplies to a food bank or women's shelter. Or challenge yourself to be an undercover good-doer: do something kind when no one's looking and keep it a total secret.

For Me

IT'S NEVER TOO LATE TO DIVE INTO THE RICH GIFTS OF HISTORY. Start with the local tourism office, and learn about heritage festivals, landmarks, and museum tours you can try. Visiting a different city? Check the bookstore or gift shops for a history of that area's shipwrecks, hauntings, or battles. Or just watch *Hamilton*! (Again.)

For You

FAMILY STORIES HELP US APPRECIATE THE CHALLENGES OUR ANCESTORS FACED and the sacrifices they made. Digging into these—and repeating them to younger generations—can help reassure us that we can prevail in tough times, too. Also share your family's *medical* history. It might help younger members live longer.

HISTORY

GRACE

For Me

FORGIVE YOURSELF. FOR ANYTHING AND EVERYTHING. Immediately, if not sooner. Because that's what you'd do for a good friend. Because it sets a good example for your loved ones. Remind yourself that people are usually doing the best they can, at any given moment. That includes you. Re-read this as often as you need to.

For You

WRITE A FORGIVENESS LETTER TO SOMEONE WHO HURT YOU. Include what happened, how you felt, and what you learned. Consider their perspective. What might have led to their actions? You don't have to send the letter, especially if they don't know you were upset in the first place. Either way, they will benefit from the results.

For Me

PLANNING A TRIP IS ALMOST AS FUN AS TAKING ONE, so go ahead and contact a travel agent. Find out what your dream vacation would cost and start saving up! For now, pack a "go bag" and renew (or apply for) your passport, so you'll be ready to go anywhere, anytime, at the drop of a sun hat!

For You

GIVE THE GIFT OF A GETAWAY. Re-create your favorite childhood vacation and take your parents or siblings along. Or rent an extra-large condo and offer a free room to friends who took a financial hit this year. No time to travel yourself? Sponsor an arts, sports, or academic trip for a high-school student. The possibilities are boundless!

I ♥ TRAVEL

GO!

WATCH

For Me

TV SEEMS LIKE A MINDLESS ESCAPE, BUT IT HAS THE POWER TO BROADEN OUR MINDS. Look at your "watch list" and add some titles that can help you enhance your living space, build new skills, understand other cultures, or laugh out loud. When viewing, check in with how you feel, and make a *mindful* decision to "keep watching" (or not).

For You

LOOK FOR WHERE YOU CAN GIVE A GIFT OF MEDIA. Is there a senior you know who would love to fill some hours with a gift of classic movies or a subscription service? Local childcare center in need of some fun, educational DVDs or software? Local library with a wish list? You can share entertainment and education.

For Me

EVEN IF YOU'RE FEELING OVEREXTENDED, YOU CAN EASILY ADD SOME STRETCHING TO YOUR DAY. Just move around in whatever way feels good. Also, try a few yoga classes (online or in person). Some instructors play Beatles songs and do handstands, while others burn incense and do deep breathing. Keep searching until you find one with your vibe.

For You

HELP OTHERS STRETCH THEIR WINGS by offering words of encouragement or physical help. Be a workout buddy for a new exerciser. Volunteer at an immigration office as a teacher or helper. Sponsor someone who's seeking to join your faith community. Or invite your extended family to start a scholarship fund. Ask your bank for help setting it up.

For Me

RISE AND SHINE! SUNLIGHT—AND LIGHT IN GENERAL—IS A NATURAL MOOD BOOSTER. Watch the sun rise. Open all your curtains. Sit by a window. Work, play, and dine outdoors. Also brighten up your *indoor* spaces: replace burned-out lightbulbs with eco-friendly ones, and add lamps to areas that need more light. (That's also easier on your eyes.)

For You

INTERESTED IN SOLAR POWER? You don't have to install solar panels to get in the game. Just switch to green electricity suppliers, which use only solar, wind, and water as power sources. Oh, and remember that tip about opening the curtains? Using natural light instead of electric is good for the planet, too.

For Me

GO AHEAD AND RUIN YOUR APPETITE! Eat dessert first or have dessert *as* your dinner once in a while. But be choosy. Lots of the goodies you loved as a kid are *not* as delicious as you remember. When you decide to indulge, visit a high-end bakery or ask a family member to make your favorite birthday cake.

For You

HERE'S A SWEET AND SIMPLE GESTURE: offer to split dessert with your friends when you go out to eat. Those first few bites are the best anyway and you won't all feel like a *Charlie and the Chocolate Factory* reject when you're done. Plus, it's a quiet way to help people who need to limit sugars but want a little taste of the good life.

Sweet

For Me

IF YOUR MORNING ROUTINE IS, WELL, ROUTINE, SHAKE IT UP! Tiny tweaks can make you more productive. Experts suggest these dos and don'ts: Don't look at your phone for 30 minutes. Do make the bed. Don't skip breakfast. Do drink a glass of water. And when you log on, don't get lost in your email in-box—read something *inspiring*!

For You

ARE YOU A MORNING PERSON? PUT YOUR PERSONALITY TO GOOD USE. Give a wake-up call to a friend before a flight. Get a side gig delivering newspapers. Take the opening shift at work. Play with your pets before work. If you're a night owl, apply the same principles to p.m. activities, so your morning person can go to bed early.

For Me

WHEN LIFE HAS NO REASON OR RHYME, POUR OUT YOUR FEELINGS IN A POEM. Look up how to write a haiku, cinquain, or limerick, or just go freestyle. For fun, use a magnetic poetry kit to create word art on your fridge. Too tired to think? Look up the lyrics to your favorite song. (That's a poem, too.) And laugh at the words you got wrong!

For You

SUPPORT POETS EVERYWHERE. Invite friends to a poetry slam. Buy poetry books as gifts. Choose an anthology for your book club. Explore styles from other cultures and time periods. And support "commercial" poetry by purchasing greeting cards, wall art, and children's books that feature this literary art.

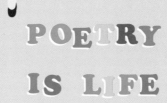

For Me

HUG IT OUT! HUGS LOWER STRESS, BOOST IMMUNITY, AND SHOW LOVE. Not a people hugger? Cuddle a cat, burp a baby, squeeze a pillow, or hug a tree. Before bed, hug *yourself* by lying down and hugging your knees to your chest for a bit. This is a great way to say "I love you" to your body.

For You

HUGGY PEOPLE TAKE NOTE: NOT EVERYONE LIKES HUGS, so always ask before you squeeze. Some people prefer an elbow tap, fist bump, or "air hug" from across the room. If *you're* not much of a hugger, don't be afraid to *say* so. Friends would rather find out *that* way than by feeling you go tense or pull back! With all of your favorite people, come up with a special show of affection that makes both of you feel great.

For Me

"WIN" AT FRIENDSHIP WITH GAME NIGHT. Bunco works with up to 12 players, and you can rotate hosts each month. Or make it like book club, changing up the game each time you gather. Bonus points for decorations, dressing up, and simple prizes. On a rainy day, have your own game day: play solitaire with *real* cards. It's soothing just to shuffle.

For You

WHO CAN YOU BLESS WITH THE GAMES YOU DON'T WANT? Consider colleges, retirement homes, shelters, children's charities, or a firehouse. Leave a game behind at a vacation rental. But keep a few classic games suitable for all ages. They're a great way to engage kids at gatherings and bring family members together across generations.

PLAY

For Me

PODCASTS ARE MAGIC. You can listen anywhere on any device, and they're easier to follow than audiobooks. Plus, you can find one on pretty much any topic. Of course, that can also be *overwhelming,* and we often fall into listening to the same perspectives over and over again. Ask some podcast fans for their top five, and try venturing outside of your usual circle of listening this week.

For You

SUPPORT THE WORK OF PODCASTERS, especially ones you know personally. Share their link on social media, be a guest, introduce them to potential interviewees, or offer help with tech or a business plan. Also, lend an ear when they want to brainstorm (or complain) about their new venture. Sometimes they just need to talk it out!

For Me

INSTEAD OF PIZZA NIGHT (*AGAIN!*), STEP OUTSIDE YOUR CULTURAL COMFORT ZONE. Try a new type of food, music, or dance. Seek artists whose backgrounds are completely different from yours. Visit museums, exhibits, and festivals that highlight a particular culture. Save tickets and pics to remind you to keep expanding your understanding.

For You

INVITE FAMILY MEMBERS TO SHARE STORIES ABOUT *YOUR* CULTURAL HERITAGE. What did they cook, wear, celebrate, sing, and read? No one to ask? No problem. Volunteer at a site where your family's culture is celebrated. You can lend a helping hand while learning more and honoring your ancestors.

SHOWER

For Me

EVERYONE DESERVES TO BE SHOWERED WITH ATTENTION! Replace your loofah (and razor). Light a scented candle. Play soothing music. Drop a shower bomb. Deep-condition your hair. Exfoliate. Sip some shower wine or coffee. (Use a lidded cup. Even fruity shampoo tastes *gross*.) When you're done, wrap up in a fluffy towel!

For You

FILL A GUEST-ROOM BASKET WITH LITTLE LUXURIES AND EVERYDAY NEEDS. Think beyond hotel toiletries to include surprises, like a candle, a facial mask, a deck of cards, single-serving snack packs, and a book. Make an extra basket or two for people who live alone. Or offer to whip up a few similar baskets for a charity raffle.

For Me

TAKING A NEW ROUTE CAN SPARK CURIOSITY and help us notice things we might otherwise miss. Drive a different road to work. Go the opposite direction on your neighborhood walk. Write with your nondominant hand. Sleep on the "wrong" side of the bed. Eat breakfast at suppertime. Who knows? This may be your new normal.

For You

CREATE A SCAVENGER HUNT FOR A FRIEND OR FAMILY MEMBER, taking them to places that carry significance for your relationship. You can make it a solo adventure with little rewards along the way or go along and watch them discover each location with you by their side—with time spent together as the best reward.

VENTURE

For Me

WE ALL LOVE A FROTHY COFFEE DRINK NOW AND THEN, BUT INVESTING IN YOUR FUTURE IS A BETTER BUY. Saving can be simple: Choose generics. Don't buy anything "big" unless you sleep on it. Cut the landline. Re-evaluate your subscriptions. And brew your own joe most days. Use the savings to max out your 401(k) or take a résumé-building class.

For You

YOUR MONEY-SAVING TRICKS CAN HELP OTHERS, TOO. Share a ride service or start a car pool. Share a phone plan with extended family members. Split a meal. Shop at a big-box store, and split the goods (and the savings). And if you're buying something you won't use often—like a power washer—go in on one with another family. It all adds up.

For Me

ENVISION YOURSELF ACHIEVING A GOAL, and you're more likely to achieve it. To focus your mind's eye, make a vision board. You can take the classic approach of clipping relevant pictures and words from magazines or search online for inspirational messaging to print. Either way, create a poster and hang it where you'll see it each day. Draw on it for inspo and update it when you find a new pic.

For You

POST ENCOURAGEMENT FOR ANOTHER ACHIEVER. Know someone walking or running a race? Create a poster to cheer them on and be there for the toughest stretch. Graduate in your circle? Share your support with a poster full of proud words and pics. Child starting first grade or a new school? Tell them, "You've got this!" in big print.

For Me

WHETHER WE LIKE TO ADMIT IT OR NOT, PHYSICAL CLUTTER AFFECTS OUR MIND AND EMOTIONS. Make a sweep through your rooms, quickly clearing the surfaces of whatever would get in the way of a vacuum or dust rag. (Collect the items in a basket to put away later.) The best part about tidying? Your space will look so nice, you might be able to push off *cleaning* by another day (or week).

For You

IF YOU'VE EVER WORKED AT A STORE, YOU KNOW HOW HARD IT IS to keep all the displays neatly stacked. You can do little things to help retail personnel stay sane. Straighten up after searching for a size, close zippers and buttons before returning clothes to the rack, and ask if you can help by removing hangers at the checkout. Let retail workers know you appreciate them.

For Me

GREETING CARDS ARE THE CLIFFSNOTES OF HAPPINESS. Anytime you need a boost, head for their aisle, and read as many as you can in 10 minutes. Buy a few for the future (or for your vision board). And keep the cards you receive in a basket or box to peruse later. Just seeing your loved ones' handwriting can bring them close, if only for a moment.

For You

DON'T WAIT FOR THE HOLIDAYS TO SEND "SEASON'S GREETINGS" TO LOVED ONES. That's such a busy time, we can barely scrawl our names on the cards! Instead, dig out your address list now, and send a few cards each month. Sip a cup of tea, compose your thoughts, then write the thoughtful note you always wanted to send.

CONNECT

QUIET

For Me

YOU DON'T NEED A CHICHI SHE SHED TO CARVE OUT A QUIET SPACE JUST FOR YOU. Choose a sunny corner of a room or a plush armchair, and claim it for a reading nook or meditation spot. Stock it with things that smell and taste sweet or that instantly spark a smile. Let others in your household know to leave you alone when you're in the zone!

For You

HONOR QUIET SPACE FOR OTHERS. Sometimes we don't think about things that might disrupt others as we go about our day. Talk with members of your household about the times they need peace and quiet and how you can support it. Consider your neighbors: try not to use loud tools when someone's having a picnic or during their baby's nap time. Timing is everything.

For Me

FOR OUR DREAMS TO BEAR FRUIT, WE NEED TO "WEED OUT" NEGATIVE THOUGHTS before they take root. As soon as one pops up, try this: Name five good things that you see and feel right now. *The sky is blue. My mouth is minty. I hear a bird. I smell freshly cut grass. The sun is warm.* When you stop and smell the roses (or the grass), you bring yourself back to the present.

For You

WEEDING FLOWER BEDS AT A FRIEND'S BUSINESS, A LOCAL CHARITY, OR A NEIGHBOR'S HOUSE is a simple way to serve others. So is keeping a garden (or indoor plants) well watered while people are away on vacation. Know a gardener who can no longer kneel to tend their beds? Set them up with planters or raised beds, which are available as kits.

TEAM

For Me

TEAMWORK MAKES THE DREAM WORK. If you haven't played sports since you were a kid, look for an amateur league, then talk to the players to see if you'd be a good fit. Even if you prefer solo sports like running, paddleboarding, or archery, you can look for a club where you can participate in tournaments—and cheer one another on.

For You

WHEN NEW MEMBERS JOIN A TEAM YOU'RE ON, DESIGNATE YOURSELF AS THE WELCOMING COMMITTEE. Talk to them about the team culture, find them a uniform or team T-shirt before the first game, and introduce them around. Think about all the things you wish you'd known when you started, then share that with them.

For Me

PAPER CLUTTER IS A SIDE EFFECT OF PROCRASTINATION, SO DEAL WITH PAPERS as soon as they come into your home. Sort them into categories: action items, to be filed, or recyclables. Also sign up for online banking, receipts, health test results, coupons, and anything else that can help you avoid leaving a paper trail through the house. You'll have more physical space, headspace, and time to put toward joy, not paper chasing.

For You

ACCORDING TO A JAPANESE TALE, MAKING 1,000 ORIGAMI CRANES WILL GRANT YOU ONE WISH. Today, the National Crane Project uses this many donated cranes to create mobiles that are displayed to raise awareness about pediatric cancer. You could also give origami art as gifts or amuse kids by folding a dollar bill into a heart or dog.

freedom

For Me

WEAR WHAT MAKES YOU FEEL FABULOUS WHEN YOU'RE WEARING IT—whether it's yoga pants or sequins or both together. Don't buy clothing just because it's on sale, it's trendy, or someone *else* says it looks good. To work through your closet, start by turning all of the hangers around so they hook from the back. After you wear something that feels great, flip it the other way to mark a keeper. Remove any pieces that don't feel like you.

For You

AS YOU WHITTLE DOWN YOUR WARDROBE TO YOUR FAVORITES, DONATE the items you're letting go to a local thrift store, a fundraising rummage sale for a local school or charity, or a nonprofit that helps people re-enter the workplace. You'll find your favorite outfits more easily in your closet while helping to clothe others in need.

For Me

MOST PEOPLE DON'T EAT ENOUGH PRODUCE, BUT IT'S EASY TO ADD A SERVING TO EACH MEAL. Stir baby spinach into your morning scrambled egg. Make a smoothie for a snack. Top your sandwich with apple and avocado slices. Coming up with new culinary ideas is also a great way to get your creative juices flowing! Treat yourself to tools that help make enjoying fruits and veggies easier.

For You

TO HELP STUBBORN EATERS EAT HEALTHIER, YOU MAY NEED TO GET A BIT SNEAKY. Replace white rice with riced cauliflower in soups or chili. Add pureed veggies to homemade meatballs or store-bought sauces. Chop extra vegetables into side salads, and switch from iceberg lettuce to spinach. Also try sweet potato fries, which almost everyone loves.

For Me

IF THERE'S A SONG IN YOUR HEART, LET IT OUT—even if you don't think you can carry a tune. Or take lessons in voice or an instrument you always wanted to play. Want something more, um, practical? Try Pound, a drumming-based workout that lets you channel your inner rock star.

For You

HIGH-FIDELITY EARPLUGS HELP TONE DOWN THE DECIBELS of ambient music without compromising sound quality. They're a great gift for performers, audience members, and families of garage bands. Get a pair for yourself, so you can support amateur musicians and singers. Your presence at a gig is the *best* present you can offer.

(117)

For Me

DO YOU GET TONGUE-TIED WHEN SOMEONE ASKS, "SO, WHAT DO YOU DO?" You need an *elevator pitch*—a description short enough to share on a quick elevator ride. Skip the job title, and instead think of *who* you help, *what* you help them do, and *how* you do that. ("I help people engage in self-care by writing quick tips in pretty books!")

For You

TO ELEVATE OTHERS, ENGAGE IN POSITIVE GOSSIP. Tell their colleagues, employers, friends, and family how specifically awesome they are. By shining a light on their best qualities, you may set them up for better relationships with others. And if they overhear that you're championing them, they'll love *you* more, too.

Peace

For Me

RELEASE THE TENSION IN YOUR BODY, ONE MUSCLE AT A TIME, with progressive muscle relaxation. Lie down on the floor, a sofa, or your bed and close your eyes. As you inhale, tense one body part (say, your hands), and hold. As you exhale, fully release the tension, letting that part "melt" into your supporting surface. Do this for every part of you. (It can also help you fall asleep.)

For You

PROMOTE A PEACEFUL WORLD, ONE BIT AT A TIME, STARTING WITH CHILDREN. Show them how to be kind to animals. Coach them to sit beside kids who are alone and lonely. Invite them to participate in or ride along when you do charitable work. Look for ways to support peaceful practices by people of all ages in your community.

For Me

TREAT YOURSELF TO AN AMAZING DINING-OUT EXPERIENCE WITH A FEW TRICKS. For more personal attention, go on a weeknight, and don't take the first or last reservation. (That's when servers are gearing up or winding down.) For the very best meal, ask the server for a few suggestions.

For You

GO BEYOND GENEROUS TIPS TO MAKE SERVERS SMILE. Set aside your phone and pay attention to the specials, so they don't have to repeat them. Be ready to clear aside space when new courses arrive at the table. Don't forget the thank-yous throughout the experience. Include a short message (along with that big tip) when you sign the receipt, and praise great service to any managers on hand.

ON THE TOWN

≫REBOOT≫

For Me

HAVE YOU REBOOTED LATELY? Adopting better tech habits can save you a megabyte of trouble in the future. Some simple tips: restart your phone, computer, and smartwatch at least once a week; back up your data; and use a password manager. Not sure how? Get help from a tech guru. Tech time-outs to reboot also give you designated space to break free from your gadgets. Don't rush back to all those refreshed screens so quickly.

For You

HELP KIDS REBOOT (LITERALLY) by contributing to a winter-boot drive at a school or nonprofit or teaching a child how to tie their shoelaces. Or help a kid reboot mentally by making sure that you'll both step away from your devices to enjoy a day on the town or out in nature together.

For Me

ADD A LITTLE MAGIC (OR MYSTERY) TO YOUR LIFE! You could seek out a street magician or go to a magic show—or you might try a little sleight of hand yourself. Pick up a kit or watch some YouTube tutorials to wow 'em at your next party. Not up for prestidigitation right now? Whip up a batch of cookies, then help them disappear.

For You

IF WE LISTEN VERY CLOSELY, WE CAN HELP MAKE LOVED ONES' WISHES COME TRUE. Make a note whenever someone expresses a desire for a particular item, and you'll never be at a loss for the perfect present. They'll think you're a mind reader! Include experiential wishes, too, like going to Disney World or trying indoor skydiving.

For Me

IF YOU LOVE SOMETHING, PROTECT IT. Avoid a house fire by cleaning out the dryer hose. Update your will and vaccinations. Above all, learn to fight for yourself, whether from a self-defense class or a martial arts program. Working toward a black belt is, in itself, a process full of challenges and rewards.

For You

DOCTOR APPOINTMENTS CAN BE CONFUSING, ESPECIALLY FOR OLDER ADULTS. Offer to be someone's "health buddy." You'd go along, take notes, ask questions, and make sure they understand any instructions. The buddy system also works well for people trying to quit bad habits (like smoking) or start good ones (like exercise).

For Me

YOU JUST WALKED INTO A ROOM AND FORGOT WHY. GOOD NEWS: YOU'RE NOT LOSING IT. The act of crossing a threshold tells your brain a new scene is starting, which makes you forget. Use this to your benefit. When you get home, pretend your worries are in a briefcase, then mentally leave it at the door (along with your shoes).

For You

TAKING OFF YOUR SHOES AT THE DOOR IS A BLESSING IN MANY WAYS. If little kids play on the floors, you're limiting their exposure to allergens, dirt, and germs. If you have downstairs neighbors, you're reducing the noise. If you're a guest, you're helping to protect your host's floor coverings.

HOLIDAY
COUNTRY
STYLE

PAUSE

For Me

IN A TECH-CENTRIC WORLD, FEASTING YOUR EYES ON A PAPER PERIODICAL CAN BE INTENSELY SATISFYING. Magazines, in particular, practically demand that you thumb through them slowly. Go to your pile of back issues or have fun at a newsstand, find a cozy chair (and maybe a cat), and dive in.

For You

IF YOUR LOVE OF BOOKS, MAGAZINES, AND JOURNALS IS CLASHING with your desire to protect the forests, do things to balance the equation. Switch from paper products to cloth napkins, dust rags, and handkerchiefs, for example. You can also make sure your books and magazines go far by donating them to a neighbor, library, school, senior day center, or hospital after your reading is complete.

For Me

FINALLY, OUR CULTURE HAS BEGUN TO EMBRACE THE IDEA OF FEELING BEAUTIFUL, JUST THE WAY YOU ARE. To help your head catch up, stop focusing on size, and set health goals instead. Try this mental exercise, too: cover sticky notes with 10 or more amazing things your body has allowed you to do, then put them all over your mirrors.

For You

SUPPORT OTHERS BY COMPLIMENTING THEM ON THINGS THAT ARE NOT PHYSICALLY FOCUSED. Do you love their laugh? Maybe they are a good listener. Perhaps they have a lot of patience. Also stop criticizing your own body in conversations. Being a model of body love can quietly help others advance on their own journey.

For Me

CHOOSING A "MANTRA" CAN FEEL HIGH-PRESSURE. For a low-key way to focus on positive words, create a word cloud. You can use a "Wordle" tool online, or just cut out or draw a shape—like a heart—and cover it with words that hold special meaning. Love it? Sandwich it between clear contact paper or run it through a laminator to preserve it.

For You

CREATE WORD CLOUDS FOR BIRTHDAY CARDS AND SPECIAL OCCASIONS. Think about the nature of the event, as well as the people being celebrated. Incorporate their names, the date, and other details to create a piece of artwork that will serve as a reminder of the celebration—and a celebration of your love.

For Me

GOT A MINUTE? THINK ABOUT THE HARDEST THING YOU HAVE TO DO (or want to do) today, then set a timer and do it for a minute. Exercise. Pay bills. Clean the toilet. Start a horrible work project. After 60 seconds, you'll find it easier to keep going. If you're still stuck, do something else for a bit, and try again.

For You

TALK ABOUT TIMING BEFORE YOU VISIT LOVED ONES. Let them know when you plan to arrive and how long you are able to stay. This can ensure they're not stressed or surprised at your arrival—and it can ease the pleas for "just one more minute," especially if they wish you could stay forever.

For Me

SET A GOAL (NO MATTER HOW BIG OR SMALL) AND DECIDE WHAT YOU'LL AWARD YOURSELF if you reach it. For example, if you want to walk more often, pick a perk (like new tunes) and treat yourself if you meet your weekly goal. It's fun to keep track with a jumbo calendar: put a sticker or star on every day you succeed.

For You

HELP SOMEONE DISPLAY THE AWARDS THEY'VE RECEIVED from work, school, or hobbies. Examples: Create a quilt from old sports or theater T-shirts. Hang some hooks to display marathon medals. Put paper certificates in frames. These are tangible ways to show your support. (Feel free to hire out or DIY.)

For Me

AT SOME POINT, WE REALIZE WE CANNOT BE ALL THINGS TO ALL PEOPLE. The next step is realizing that's *awesome*. Maybe you forget birthdays, but you write thoughtful notes in (belated) cards. Maybe you bake homemade cakes. Or maybe it's best when you *don't*. If you *want* to be a better baker, find a way to foster that skill. But only if it matters to *you*. Focus on the areas that reward your soul

For You

HERE'S THE FRINGE BENEFIT OF NOT TRYING TO EMULATE every friend, family member, and TV personality in the world: it allows you to *truly* celebrate the people who are fabulous at your worst skills. Let them know how much you appreciate their unique gifts. You could even create a cheat sheet of sorts that lists everyone in your circle and the talents they're happy to share.

For Me

THE FAIRY TALE WE WROTE FOR OURSELVES AS LITTLE KIDS MAY NOT HAVE PLAYED OUT as planned. Take a beat, and decide if you still *want* to write the great American novel—or if you just liked the idea of it. If it's the latter, let it go. If you're not sure, explore. Take a class, talk to people in the field . . . then go for it or let it go.

For You

THINK ABOUT WHAT SPARKED YOUR CHILDHOOD DREAMS. If you wanted to be a detective because you love solving things, maybe you could open an escape room for like-minded people. Or perhaps you could be a forensic accountant, figuring out cases of fraud. When we're passionate about our work, we can't help but improve the world.

For Me

FACING OUR FEARS CAN HELP US BE BRAVE IN THE FUTURE—and often, we find things aren't as scary as they seem. When you start to feel pushback, use it as your signal to *go*. Try ziplining or waterskiing. Eat sushi or chocolate crickets. Pick a fear (any fear) and face it ASAP. Above all, *don't* fear failure. It's a stepping-stone to success—or at least discovery.

For You

FIGHTING OUR OWN DEMONS CAN HELP US BE BRAVE WHEN LOVED ONES ARE STRUGGLING with a crisis or loss, big or small. Think of all the ways you might calm a fearful child: Rub their back. Speak in a calm tone. And remind them that they have prevailed over challenges in the past. Having done it once, they can do it again.

BRAVE

For Me

WHEN YOU STEP INTO NATURE, LOOK FOR HEART SHAPES. You'll be surprised at how often this motif appears, from your backyard to vacation locales. Searching is a fun way to really focus your attention on the flora and fauna, rocks and trees, sky and sea, or whatever is around you. Snap pictures to use as a screen saver or wall art.

For You

SEEK LOVE IN EVERYONE YOU MEET. The ornery relative. The smart-mouthed kid. The sour-faced clerk. Look for their heart—try to see their best qualities, even if they're tucked away. There are things we can all agree on, even if we don't agree on how to get there. If we can focus on what's at heart, that's a good start.

For Me

THINK ABOUT WHAT ENCOURAGING MESSAGE YOU NEED to hear the most right now. Write it on a sticky note in bright, bold lettering, then post it where you can see it at the start and finish of the day. Revisit your affirmation at least once each week to decide if it needs updating.

For You

WRITE CHALK MESSAGES ON YOUR DRIVEWAY TO INSPIRE OTHERS—or to at least inspire smiles. If you're sure it would be a welcome gesture, share encouraging words by chalking another person's driveway on a birthday, an anniversary, or any random day you want to brighten. The act will make you feel like a carefree kid again, too.

For Me

CHOOSE A NEW HANDS-ON CRAFT TO LEARN, whether it's knitting, creating pottery, or making jewelry. Take a class, watch tutorials, or ask a talented friend to help you catch on. Then grant yourself permission to simply enjoy the process and not focus on the result. Make yourself something that's beautiful in your eyes because of the heart that went into the creation.

For You

FIND A WAY YOUR NEW CRAFT CAN BLESS OTHERS, once you're comfortable sharing your creations. Knit little blankets to be donated to your local animal shelter or little preemie hats for your local hospital. Make jewelry for women in need who are re-entering the workforce. You can also offer to teach a child in your life the skill you just learned.

For Me

THINK ABOUT THE NEXT HOLIDAY ON THE CALENDAR. What do you love most about how you celebrate? Make a mental note to elevate that element to the top. What stresses you out? Either cut that part out completely or consider a way to simplify what you usually do. Take control of your celebration, and you'll rediscover joy.

For You

CONSIDER WHO MAY FEEL LEFT OUT OR HURT ON THIS HOLIDAY. A widow or widower on Valentine's Day? Someone struggling with infertility on Mother's or Father's Day? A neighbor alone at Christmas? Extend an act of kindness—even if it's simply a "thinking of you" card or a moment of listening.

For Me

LOOK AT YOUR TYPICAL DAY AND FIND A FEW PLACES WHERE YOU CAN INSERT A PAUSE. Resolve to step away from the rushing and racing, even if just for a few moments. Slow down to simply take a breath, meditate, pray, text a loved one how grateful you are for them...whatever centers you.

For You

THROUGHOUT YOUR DAY, CONSIDER TIMES WHEN YOU CAN STEP ASIDE TO HELP OTHERS. Parent with a young child waiting in line? Let them go ahead of you. Someone struggling to make a tough turn out of a parking lot? Give them space to pull out in front of your car. One seat left in the convenience restaurant or one bench left in the park? Check that no one else more in need is waiting.

For Me
&
For You

WITHOUT THE EBB, WE WOULDN'T APPRECIATE THE FLOW. Whatever challenges you're facing, remember that all you need to do is ride them out. Let yourself feel all the feels—fear, exhilaration, grief, or a swirl of emotions. Remember that, in time, these will crest, crash, and recede. Turn to others for help, and be their source of support when you're riding high and they're treading water.

Smoother sailing and sunnier skies lie ahead—if only we care for one another.

TOGETHER

In our togetherness, castles are built.

—IRISH PROVERB